INTRODUCTION

The things that we believe are like seeds
that we plant in our hearts.

Our hearts are like fertile soil that grow
whatever is planted in them.

So if we plant destructive seeds, we get
horrible trees growing in our hearts and
minds, producing bad fruit in our lives.

But if we plant seeds of God's truth about
who we are and who He is, we will find
ourselves in the most beautiful
garden, bearing good fruit
that lasts for generations
to come.

HOW TO USE THIS BOOK

Take this bag of seeds (book)

Put them in your mouth (speak them outloud): One at a time, chewing slowly, or all at once for a feast.

'Chew the cud' - munching on the seeds throughout the day; on the bus, on the loo, feeding your children, or your goldfish.

Notice which ones are harder to swallow. Ask the Holy Spirit to help you understand why.

Ask Jesus to take out all of the old destructive thoughts - weeds that want to choke these precious seeds - and make a decision to help Him.

Plant the seed firmly in your heart and water it often - declaring the truth outloud or whilst looking in the mirror

WATCH IT "GROW"

Take some seeds
from the plants
in your new
garden and
give them
to a friend.

5

I am God's very good idea

I am fearfully and wonderfully made

I am the apple of God's eye

I am God's masterpiece

I am unique

I am outrageously loved

I am made in the image of God

I am born again

I am a new creation

I am pleasing to my heavenly Father

I am not alone

I am hidden under the shadow
of God's wings

I am a child of God

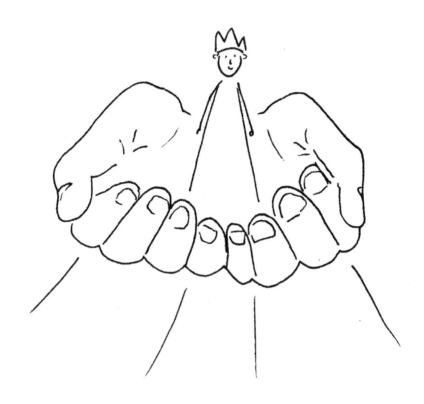

I am engraved on the palms
of God's hands

I am God's special treasure

I am covered in the blood of Jesus

I am washed whiter than snow

I am covered by grace

I am free from the law

I am free from sin

I am holy, blameless, without
reproach

I am righteous before God

I am God's dream raised from
the dead

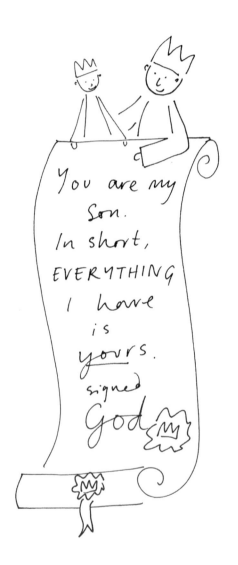

I am a coheir with Christ

I am adopted into God's family

I am refreshed in God's presence

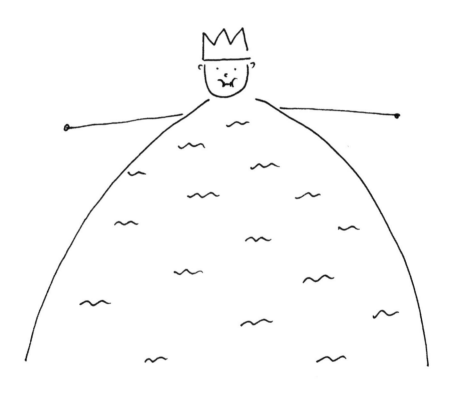

I am full of the Holy Spirit

I am overflowing with the Holy Spirit

I am on fire

I am leaning on God

I am surrendered to the will of God

I am a house built on the rock

I am seated with Christ in
heavenly places

I am clothed in my full
spiritual armour

74

I am being transformed by the renewing
of my mind

I am full of hope

I am enough just as I am

I am a blessing

I am awesome

I am a work in progress

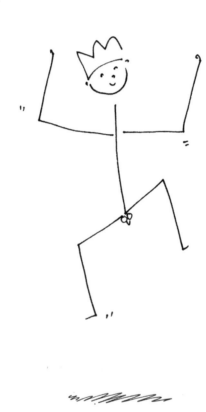

I am unashamed

I am a freedom bringer

THANK YOU
THANK YOU
THANK YOU
THANK YOU
THANK YOU
THANK YOU
THANK YOU
THANK YOU
THANK YOU
THANK YOU
THANK YOU
THANK YOU
THANK YOU
THANK YOU
THANK YOU

I am grateful

I am strong

I am childlike

I am adventurous

I am a generous and cheerful giver

I am patient

HURRY UP

I am full of wonder

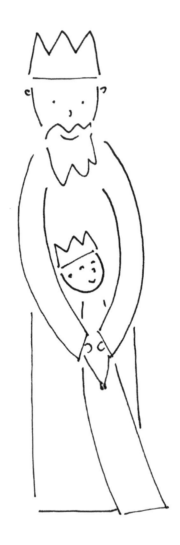

I am held by God

I am an encovrager

I am a leader

I am passionate

I am an empowerer

I am a good listener

I am a joy bringer

I am a winner

I am a worshipper

I am a shining star in a crooked
and depraved generation

I am self-controlled

I am full of good ideas

HA HA HAA

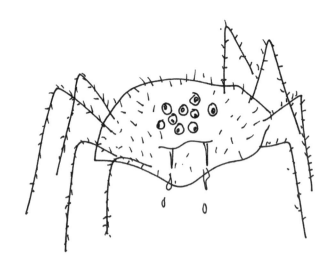

I am courageous

I am a storm-sleeper

I am an overcomer

I am in the world but not of it

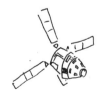

I am in two places at the same time

I am a citizen of heaven

I am Christ's ambassador

I am God's residence here on earth

I am an alien

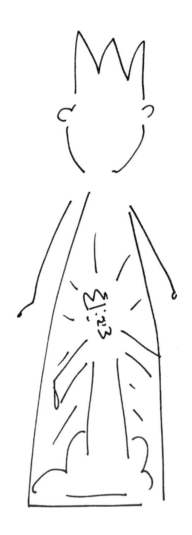

I am a portal to heaven

I am called

I am yielded to the Holy Spirit

I am a royal priest

154

I am a supernatural being with a
supernatural inheritance

I am annointed with the Holy Spirit and fire

I am equipped for every good work

I am God's messenger

I am a bringer of good news

I am a truth-teller

I am Christ's hands and feet

I am annointed to heal the sick

I am sent to bind up the
brokenhearted

I am a protector

I am able to trample on snakes
and scorpions

I am an exorcist

I am a dead raiser (funeral wrecker)

ɔɔɔɔT

I am content in all circumstances

HmlH

I am free from me

I am free from the fear of man

BOG OFF

I am free to run my race

I am free from comparing myself
with others

I am a man of my word

I am dependable

I am free from fear

I am a Holy Ghost party

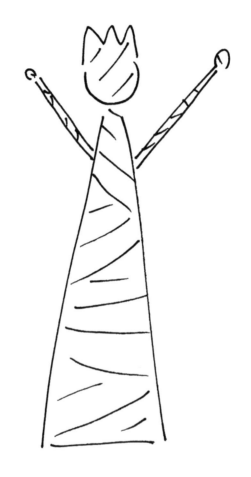

I am shrink-wrapped in the
Holy Spirit

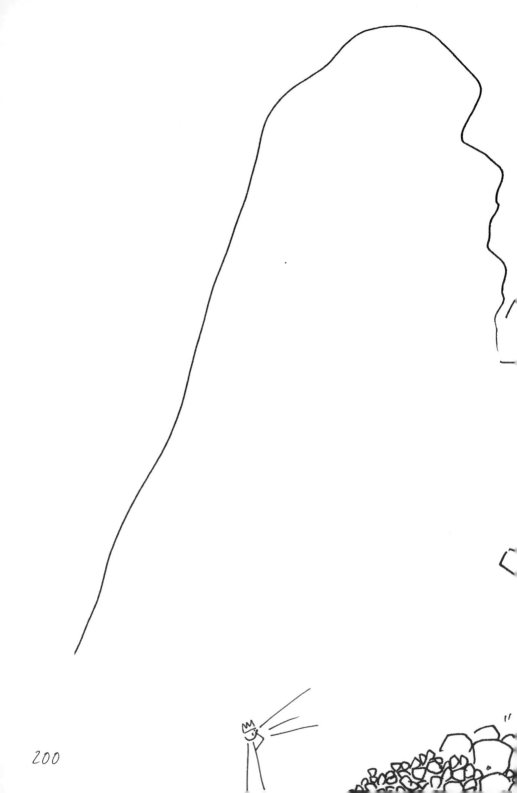

I am a mountain leveller

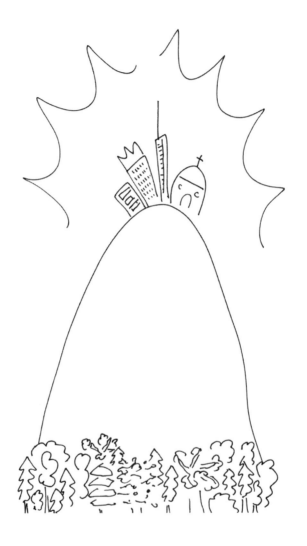

I am a city on a hill

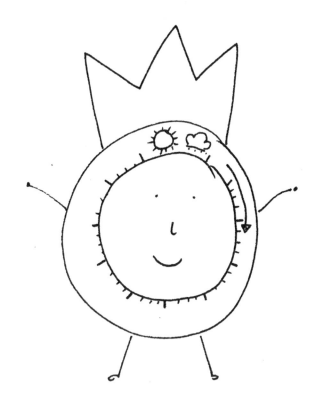

I am a thermostat
(not a thermometer)

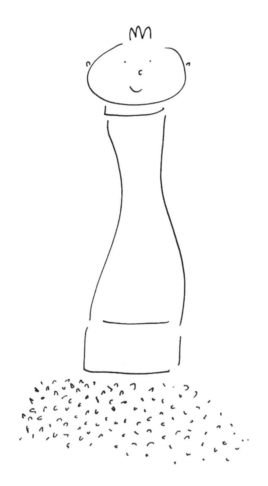

I am salty

I am unoffendable

I am an eager learner

I am in the river of life

I am rooted in Christ

I am bearing good fruit

I am an oak of righteousness

I am carrying the heart of God

I am led by the Holy Spirit

I am a risk taker

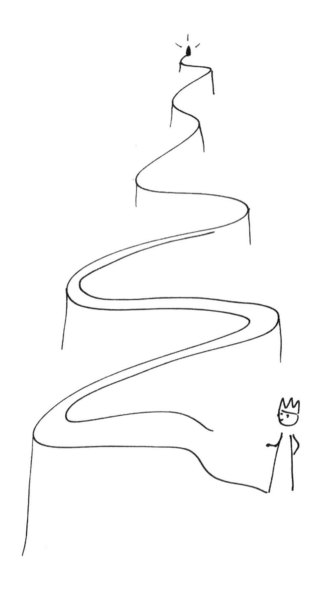

I am walking the narrow road

I am relying on God

I am my Beloved's and He is mine

I am Jesus' prize

PRAYER FROM THE AUTHOR

Papa,

Thank you for this time with the precious person who has read this book.

Thank you for the opportunity to share the gems that you are forming in me on my journey; from shame to authenticity, from hopelessness to hope, from performance to the peace of simply being your beloved daughter.

Thank you for being so kind, gentle and patient with me. Thank you for all of the help that you send our way- the friends, sermons, books, bible verses and nudges of the Holy Spirit.

I pray that the Holy Spirit will help the reader of this book to find their way into true identity and become the fullest version of who you made them to be; wherever they are at today.

Embrace the man, woman, boy or girl who has read this book. Bathe them in your love and hold them close. Bring them home, into your family, where they may know how much you love and delight in them and the abundant hope that you have for their future.

May all that has been lost and stolen be restored seven fold.
May all that has died come back to life.
May they be filled with grace, joy and peace for the journey.

In Jesus' name, Amen.

237

238

dedicated to my gorgeous husband Dom; who has cheered me on in the identity journey and without whom this book wouldn't have been possible. x

ISBN 978-0-9957941-0-8

Printed in the United Kingdom

To find out more please visit iamsomanythings.com